WHAT

MAKES OUR
EARTH UNIQUE?

Om
KIDZ

An imprint of Om Books International

Contents

What is a galaxy made of?

Stars, dust, and dark matter, all held together by gravity! A galaxy contains planets, star systems, star clusters and types of interstellar clouds. In between them is a sparse interstellar medium of gas, dust and cosmic rays. Some galaxies may also contain objects like Quasars, the most energetic bodies in the universe, at their cores.

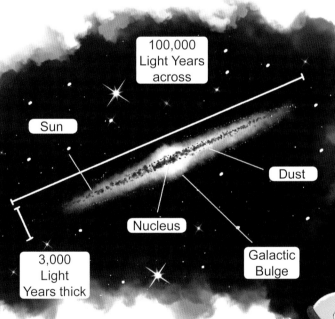

100,000 Light Years across

Sun

3,000 Light Years thick

Nucleus

Dust

Galactic Bulge

Pocket fact

Starburst!
Some galaxies form new stars rapidly. These galaxies are called Starburst. They are usually formed after large amounts of molecular clouds are produced when two galaxies merge.

What gives our galaxy its milky appearance?

Its stars! Our galaxy appears as a dim glowing band arching across the night sky. This is where most stars are located which gives it that fuzzy milky appearance. This is why our galaxy is called the Milky Way Galaxy.

Try this

Can you identify these three types of galaxies?

What is the solar system?

It's the Sun's family! The solar system consists of the Sun with its eight planets: Mercury, Venus, Earth, Mars, Jupiter, Saturn, Uranus and Neptune orbited by more than 140 moons. The solar system also has asteroids, meteors, comets, dwarf planets and other space objects orbiting the Sun. With Sun at its centre, our solar system is always in motion.

Pocket fact

Sun is orbiting too!
The Sun and our solar system have orbited the Milky Way galaxy less than 20 times in about 4.6 billion years, ever since our solar system was born. It has made 1/1250 of a revolution since the origin of humans.

Find out

Which is the oldest known star in the solar system?

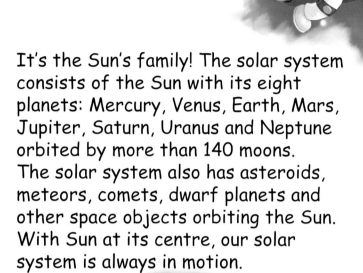

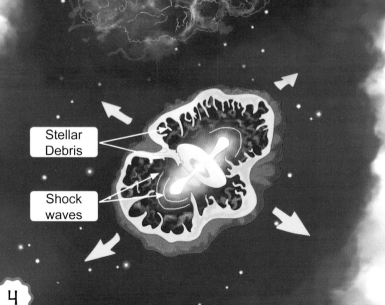

Hydrogen

Stellar Debris

Shock waves

What is a nebula?

It is where stars begin their life! A nebula is a cloud made of dust and gases, stars are formed when a nebula collapses under its own gravity. It is mainly made of hydrogen and helium. Nebulae look like fluffy clouds that are many light years away from our Earth.

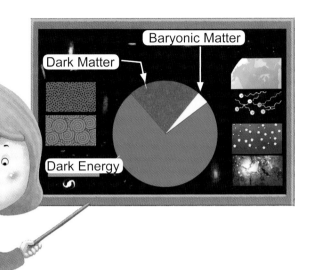

Four percent baryonic matter, 23% dark matter and 73% dark energy! Baryonic matter i.e. protons, neutrons and electrons, make everything in the universe, including the planets, stars and our Earth. Dark matter has an effect on stars and planets but we cannot see it. Dark energy is the opposite of gravity, it pushes everything away, thus expanding the universe.

Pocket fact

Nearest neighbour!
Our nearest neighbour in space, Proxima Centauri is 4.3 light years away—which is about a hundred million times farther than a trip to the Earth's moon. To reach it by a spaceship would take at least 25,000 years!

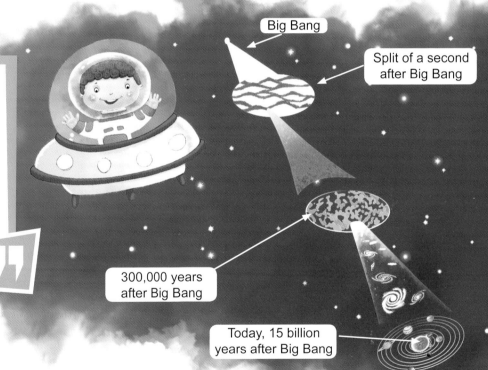

Find out

Who was the first man to look into space with a telescope?

What is the Big Bang?

A theory that explains the birth of the universe. The Big Bang theory explains that our universe exploded about 14 billion years ago. This explosion produced matter and energy. At that time, it was dense and extremely hot. The universe grew and temperatures cooled down, and eventually galaxies, stars and other heavenly bodies were formed.

What is inside the Sun?

Mostly hydrogen and helium! Other than hydrogen and helium, the Sun also has iron, nickel, oxygen, silicon, sulfur, magnesium, carbon, neon, calcium and chromium. From outside to inside, our Sun has different layers: the corona, chromosphere, photosphere and core along with sunspots and prominences.

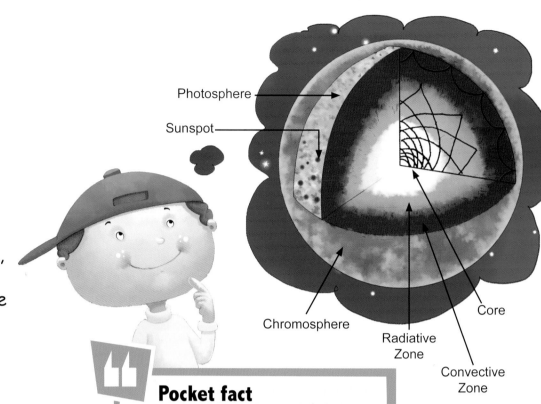

Photosphere

Sunspot

Chromosphere

Radiative Zone

Core

Convective Zone

> ## Pocket fact
>
> **Sun reverses!**
> Approximately every 11 years, the Sun reverses its overall magnetic polarity. In such a case, its North magnetic pole becomes the South pole, and vice versa.

Find out
What kind of a star is the Sun?

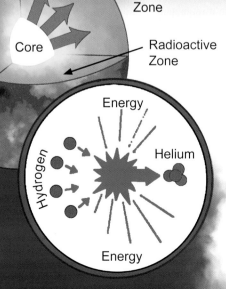

Connective Zone

Core

Radioactive Zone

Energy

Helium

Hydrogen

Energy

What is the Sun's fuel?

It's hydrogen! Hydrogen atoms collide with each other under extreme heat in the interior of the Sun and form helium molecules. The fusion of hydrogen to form helium is called nuclear fusion. It takes a million years for the energy from a single nuclear fusion reaction in the centre of the Sun to reach the surface to light up the solar system.

Cratered Surface

Lunar Seas

Lunar Highlands

What is our Moon made of?

Rocks and minerals! The composition of Moon is similar to Earth. Our Moon is mainly made of three kinds of igneous rocks: basalt, anorthosites and breccias. Astronauts also found three minerals that are not found on the Earth: armalocolite, tranquillityite and pyroxferroite.

Pocket fact

Only walked on by 12 people!
The first man to land on the Moon in 1969 was Neil Armstrong on the Apollo 11 mission, while the last man to walk on the Moon in 1972 was Eugene Cernan on the Apollo 17 mission. Since then, the Moon has only been visited by unmanned vehicles.

Find out

Which was the first spacecraft sent to Moon?

What makes the Moon shine?

Sunlight! The Moon does not have any light of its own like the Sun and the stars. It shines when its surface reflects the sunlight falling on it. Sunlight hits the dark and bumpy surface of the Moon and about 12% of it gets reflected and gives Moon its glow at night.

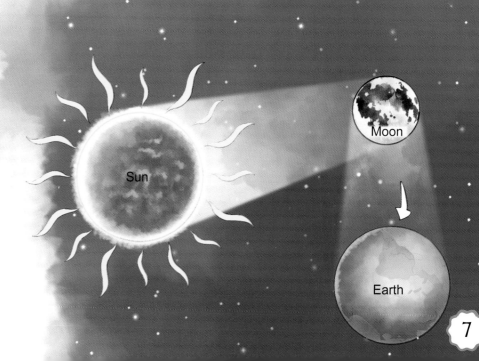

Sun

Moon

Earth

Mercury

Venus

Earth

Mars

Jupiter

Saturn

Neptune

Uranus

Sun and something more! All the eight planets of our solar family orbit the Sun, they are all nearly spherical in shape, they have the necessary mass for self-gravity that helps the planets push other celestial bodies away from their orbits.

Try this

Arrange the planets listed below in their correct order from the Sun. Venus, Jupiter, Saturn, Mercury, Earth, Uranus, Mars, Neptune.

Pocket fact

I am the fastest!
Jupiter is the fastest spinning planet in our solar system. It rotates, on an average, once in just 10 hours. This also means that Jupiter has the shortest days of all the planets in the solar system.

Water

Oxygen,

Plants & animals breathe in oxygen

Sun

150 million kms

Earth

Moon

What makes our Earth unique?

Life! Our home, Earth, is the only planet to have water and oxygen that support life. It is also at the right distance from the Sun, making it neither too hot nor too cold, and has a thick layer of atmosphere that acts as a protective cover. Not to forget our Moon, that deflects comets and meteors that might otherwise impact Earth!

What makes Venus look so bright?

Reflection of light! Venus is blanketed by a thick layer of clouds in its atmosphere. These clouds contain droplets of acidic crystals in a mixture of gases. About 70% of the sunlight falling on the planet is reflected by these crystals. This is what makes Venus look so bright in the night sky.

Reflected back to space

~460° at surface

96% CO_2

Incoming Solar Radiation

9

Pocket fact

First trip to Venus!
Venera 7 was the first spacecraft to land on Venus on December 15, 1970. It was an unmanned Soviet spacecraft. It measured the temperature of the atmosphere on Venus.

Try this

Let's spot Venus! To spot this bright planet, look towards where the Sun has just set and then look up. Even when the sky is still a deep twilight blue, you'll see a dazzling white Venus.

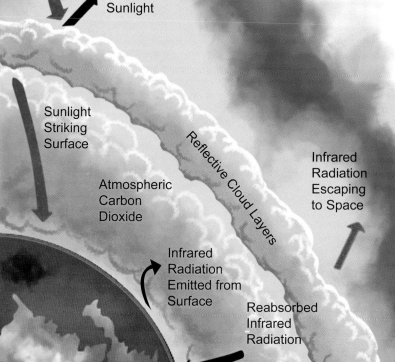

Incoming Sunlight

Reflected Sunlight

Sunlight Striking Surface

Atmospheric Carbon Dioxide

Reflective Cloud Layers

Infrared Radiation Escaping to Space

Infrared Radiation Emitted from Surface

Reabsorbed Infrared Radiation

What has made Venus the hottest planet in the solar system?

Its atmosphere! Venus' atmosphere is mainly made of carbon dioxide, and thick clouds of sulfuric acid! The atmosphere traps energy from the Sun along with the heat released by the planet. This makes the surface and the lower atmosphere of Venus one of the hottest in the solar system!

Try this

A day on Mercury is 2.45 times a day on Earth. If an Earth day=24 hours, how long is a day on Mercury? Calculate!

What gives Mercury its wrinkles?

Millions of years ago, Mercury's core cooled and contracted. The core, made of iron, gave the planet's rocky crust a wrinkly appearance. Scientists call these wrinkles Lobate Scarps. These scarps can be hundreds of kilometers in length and about two kilometres in height!

Mercury Ridge-Wrinkles

Pocket fact

The Romans named me!
Mercury was named after the Roman messenger god Mercury because it is the fastest planet. According to a myth, the messenger god had a winged hat and sandals, so he could fly.

What makes temperatures so extreme on Mercury?

Absence of a thick atmosphere! Mercury has little to no atmosphere to help regulate the temperature. During the day (i.e. when Mercury faces the Sun) temperature can reach about 8000° Fahrenheit. On the other hand, the temperature during night (on the side that doesn't face the Sun) can drop to almost -300° Fahrenheit.

What would it be like to live on Mars?

It would be very different from living on Earth! Life on Mars is not possible, but if you were there, you could experience: days 40 minutes longer than Earth's, year twice as long as Earth's, winter and summer season similar to Earth due to Mars' tilted axis. The dust in the Martian air makes the daytime sky orange whereas sunrise and sunset would be blue!

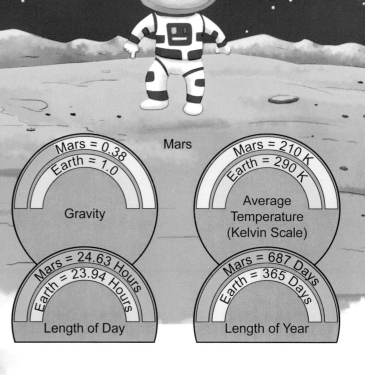

Mars

Mars = 0.38	Mars = 210 K
Earth = 1.0	Earth = 290 K
Gravity	Average Temperature (Kelvin Scale)
Mars = 24.63 Hours	Mars = 687 Days
Earth = 23.94 Hours	Earth = 365 Days
Length of Day	Length of Year

North Polar Cap

What is the story of water on Mars?

Yes, some water is there! It is frozen under the North and South polar ice caps of Mars. NASA's robotic Mars lander spacecraft, Phoenix, was the first mission to touch the frozen water in the Martian arctic in 2008. It also observed snow falling from clouds as confirmed by Mars Reconnaissance Orbiter.

Pocket fact

Longer years!
Mars' year is longer than Earth's. That's because it takes Mars 687 days to make one trip around the Sun, as opposed to Earth's 365.25 days long year. This is due to Mars' distance from the Sun.

Try this

Mars years are almost double of Earth years. If you get a chance to name the months of a Martian year, what names would you give them?

What is between Mars and Jupiter?

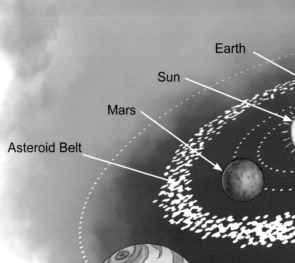

Earth

Sun

Mars

Asteroid Belt

Jupiter

An asteroid belt! It is around 2.2 to 3.2 Astronomical Units (AU) from the Sun. Asteroids are small, rocky bodies that orbit the Sun between the planets Mars and Jupiter. They mainly consist of materials left over after the formation of Mercury, Venus, Earth and Mars, the inner solar system planets.

Pocket fact

Snowman!
There is a chain of three craters on the largest asteroid called Vesta. These three craters have been nicknamed Snowman because of the shape they form!

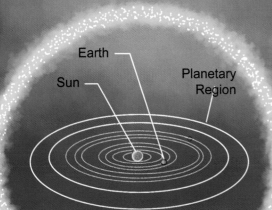

Earth

Sun

Planetary Region

Oort Cloud

What is the Oort Cloud?

The Oort Cloud is a spherical shell of trillions of frozen objects that exist in the outermost reaches of the solar system. It occupies space from 5000 to 50,000 AU (with 1 AU being the distance from the Sun to the Earth). It is named after astronomer Jan Oort, who first theorized its existence.

Find out

Which are the two spacecrafts studying Mars' atmosphere?

What is the Cassini Division of Saturn's rings?

It's a huge gap! Saturn's ring system has gaps throughout it, but Cassini Division is the largest gap in the rings of the planet. The scarcity of ring material in that gap makes it look like a dark, empty space, but in reality it is filled with ice, rocks and dust particles. The Cassini Division is about 3,000 miles or 4,800 kilometers wide and is caused by the gravitational pull from Saturn's moon—Mimas.

A ring

Cassini's Division

B ring

C ring

Pocket fact

More moons than any other planet! Saturn has at least 150 moons and moonlets. Out of these, 53 have been given official names. Imagine what the night sky would look like with 150 moons if you were on Saturn!

Try this

Make a model of Saturn using materials that can float on water just like the planet!

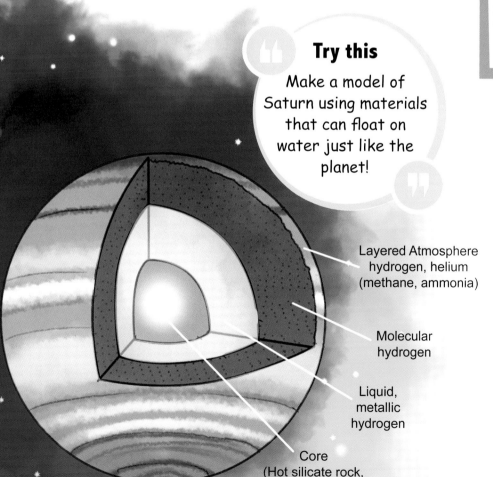

Layered Atmosphere hydrogen, helium (methane, ammonia)

Molecular hydrogen

Liquid, metallic hydrogen

Core (Hot silicate rock, maybe solid)

What makes Saturn so light?

The secret is helium! Have you seen helium gas balloons that fly high in the air? While most of the outer planets are made of a combination of hydrogen, helium and water, Saturn is mostly made of helium. This is what makes Saturn so light that it could float on water!

What makes Uranus different from other members of the solar system?

Its unusual tilt! Uranus' axis is tilted at an angle of 98°, which means that it rotates on its side. Because of this, Uranus' poles point at the Sun for half of its year. In other words, it is daytime for 42 continuous Earth years on one hemisphere, while it is night time on the other at the same time!

Sun

Uranus

Pocket fact

Only once!
Only one spacecraft has ever made a close approach to Uranus. NASA's Voyager 2 zipped past Uranus in January 1986, coming within 81,000 kms of the surface of Uranus!

Find out

When is Neptune's birthday? Which special day is dedicated to Neptune and why?

Neptune

What causes the stormy weather on Neptune?

The clash of heat and cold! Neptune gets very little heat from the Sun and has seasons just like Earth. Its great storms are caused when the internal heat from deep inside the planet, clashes with the icy cold space surrounding it.

What are meteoroids?

Meteoroids are pieces of stone-like debris that are found in outer space. They can be as small as dust particles to as big as around 10 metres in diameter. Most meteoroids are made of silicon and oxygen, minerals called silicates, and heavier metals like nickel and iron.

Pocket fact

November shower!
Every November, a meteor shower called the Leonids can be seen in the night sky. This happens when Earth moves into the thousands of fragments left behind by the Comet Tempel-Tuttle.

Find out

Who was the first person to start studying about meteors?

Meteoroid

Trail of melted pieces

Meteoroid falling on Earth

What happens when meteors rush through Earth's atmosphere?

It becomes a shooting star! When a meteoroid passes through Earth's atmosphere, it heats up due to the resistance in air. This heat causes gases around the meteoroid to glow brightly. This glowing meteoroid is called a meteor, commonly known as a shooting star!

Index